KU-719-686

GOOD
& BAD

# Bully

First published in 2007 by Cherrytree Books,
a division of the Evans Publishing Group
2A Portman Mansions
Chiltern St
London W1U 6NR

Design. D.R.ink

British Library Cataloguing in Publication Data
Amos, Janine
      Bully – (Good & Bad Series)
      I. Title II. Green, Gwen III. Series
      371.58

ISBN 1 84234 393 9
13 –digit ISBN (from 1 Jan 2007) 978 1 84234 393 7

# Bully

By Janine Amos

Illustrated by Gwen Green

CHERRYTREE BOOKS

# Michael's story

Michael was on the soccer pitch. His team was losing. And it was nearly the end of the game. Just then Michael saw his chance. He moved in to tackle. His feet did just what he wanted, and soon he had the ball. Michael knew he was playing well. He felt great!

"Peep!" went the whistle. Michael stopped in surprise.

"Foul!" the teacher called, running over. "Free kick!"

"It wasn't a foul!" said Michael truthfully.

"Don't argue, Michael," shouted the teacher, puffing, "or I'll send you off!"

Michael put his head down. Every game Mr Hicks told him off for something. He kicked at a lump of mud. "It's not fair," he muttered. His eyes were stinging with tears.

At the final whistle, Michael stamped into the changing rooms.
The boys were tugging at their shirts and racing for the showers.

"Mr Hicks is always picking on me," Michael grumbled.

"Oh, stop moaning," said another boy. "Forget it."

But Michael couldn't forget it. He pulled open his locker door
with a crash.

**How do you think Michael is feeling?**

Michael grabbed his towel and headed for the shower. But all the showers were taken. Michael felt even crosser.

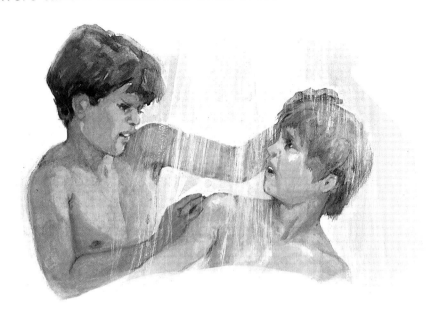

Under one shower was a very small boy. Michael glared at him.

"Hurry up!" shouted Michael. He gave the boy a big push. "Get out of my way!"

The little boy was startled. He banged his knee on the wall. It hurt a lot.

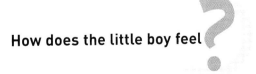

**How does the little boy feel?**

Michael felt bad. He hadn't meant to push that hard. Michael turned the shower on full. He let the water splash down on his head. "Roll on home time!" he said to himself.

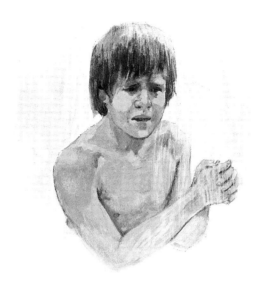

As Michael was dressing, James Russell came over. James was older than Michael. He was the school's top goalie.

"Hi!" smiled Michael. He liked James a lot.

But James didn't smile back.

"That little boy is crying," said James. "You're a bully."

Michael went bright red.

**How does Michael feel now?**

Michael told James about the football game. "Mr Hicks made me cross," he said. "Every week it's the same. He picks on me – and it's not fair."

"That doesn't mean you can pick on someone else," said James.

**Is James right?**

"Things aren't always fair," James went on. "But that's no excuse for being a bully."

"I know," said Michael quietly.

James smiled at him. "You could talk about Mr Hicks with your mum and dad. If he really does pick on you, they'll know what to do."

James waited while Michael packed his bag. Michael was still thinking about his teacher.

"Mr Hicks is a bully," he said at last. "And he made me a bully, too."

"Maybe someone's bullying him!" said James.

"That's no excuse," said Michael.

"Right!" laughed James.

**How did James help Michael**

## Feeling like Michael

Have you ever been a bully like Michael? Have you ever felt so cross that you took it out on someone weaker than yourself? However cross and upset you feel, there's no excuse for making others feel bad.

## All kinds of bullies

There are all kinds of bullies. Some bullies frighten others by shouting at them. Some push, punch or hit. Or they hurt people with unkind words or cruel jokes. Sometimes they ask for sweets or money. Many bullies are older and stronger than the people they pick on. Adults can be bullies, too.

## Talking about it

If someone bullies you, tell on them. Talk to an adult you trust. If you are a bully, you need help, too. Find an adult you can talk to. Ask them to help you stop bullying.

## Thinking about it

Read the stories in this book. Think about the people in the stories. Do you feel like them sometimes? If you're a bully or if you are being bullied, who can you tell? Talk to someone now – just as Michael did.

# Sharon's story

Sharon was sitting high on the school wall. She kicked her feet hard against the stone. Bang, bang, bang went Sharon.

Kate and Lindsey were standing nearby.

"Let's do something," said Lindsey. "I'm bored."

"Wait!" said Sharon. "Here she is!"

A little girl was walking across the playground. She was carrying a huge schoolbag. When she saw Sharon, she began to hurry away.

"Bag lady, bag lady!" called Sharon.

The girl started to run. But Sharon was too quick for her.

"What's in the bag today – the crown jewels?" said Sharon, nastily. She went right up to the little girl.

The girl looked up into Sharon's face. She felt very, very small.

The little girl cuddled her schoolbag tightly. She looked around for help. But Sharon stood in front of her, laughing. The girl's eyes filled up with tears.

"Cry baby! Bag lady!" yelled Sharon. She tugged the bag out of the girl's arms.

"Catch!" called Sharon, throwing the bag to Lindsey. Lindsey caught it – and passed it to Kate. Round and round the bag went. At last Sharon threw the bag to the ground. It landed in a puddle. The little girl bent over her schoolbag. It was covered in mud.

**How do you think the little girl feels?**

Sharon looked down at the girl, crying in the mud.

"Wait until next time," Sharon warned. She felt big and strong. She didn't feel a bit sorry.

At lunchtime, Miss Rice came over. "Come with me, please, Sharon," said the teacher.

Sharon sighed. "Another telling off," she thought. But Sharon was wrong. Miss Rice led her to an old patch of ground next door to the school.

"I want your help, Sharon," said the teacher. "I want to make a wildlife garden – with a pond."

Sharon looked at the piles of rubbish and the mud.

At break the next day, Sharon went to the garden. Some other girls were working there already, but Miss Rice worked alongside Sharon. Soon they were pulling up weeds and old barbed wire. Sharon started to enjoy herself.

"This isn't a reward for bullying, Sharon," said Miss Rice after a while. "The bullying must stop."

Sharon pretended to be busy digging. But really she was listening hard.

"You're unhappy at home just now," went on Miss Rice. "You've got a new baby sister – called Amy – haven't you?"

Sharon went red. How on earth did Miss Rice know?

"You must feel a bit left out. Amy gets all the attention," said Miss Rice.

"No one has any time for me," said Sharon.

"I have – but you've got to help yourself," said Miss Rice quickly. "Bullying might make you feel powerful at the time. But it doesn't in the long run. The good feeling doesn't last, does it?"

"No," said Sharon sadly.

Every day Sharon worked in the garden. Miss Rice lent her some books on ponds. And Sharon made the pond her project. Sometimes the other girls asked her what to do. Together they pushed three big rocks into the pond.

"They're for the frogs to jump on," said Sharon.

By spring the pond was finished. It looked great. Sharon lay on her tummy, hunting for tadpoles.

"One day Amy will see this pond. We'll tell her that her sister helped to build it," said Miss Rice.

"I never thought of that!" said Sharon, smiling.

**How did Miss Rice help Sharon?**

## Feeling bad

There are lots of reasons why people bully. They may be angry. Sometimes they are sad and jealous, like Sharon. Sometimes they are scared or hurt. Often bullies aren't the strong people they seem. Often they are lonely and afraid inside. Whatever reasons bullies have, they must stop bullying. They have no right to spoil things for others.

## Feeling good

Sharon was lucky, Miss Rice saw that she had a problem. She helped Sharon to work with others – instead of against them. She helped her to feel good about herself. If you're a bully, find someone to help you. Talk to an adult you trust. Ask them to help you stop bullying and find another way to feel important.

# Li's story

It was the summer holidays. Li had been skateboarding with the others. Now it was getting late and they were on their way home.

"There's that new kid again!" said Martin, pointing. Everyone looked at the boy coming through the park gates. "Let's get him!" called Martin.

"Oh, no," groaned Li. He watched Martin run over to the boy.

"Give me your money!" called Martin. The boy put his head down and hurried on.

"I'm talking to you!" shouted Martin.

The boy looked up. Li saw that he was frightened.

Li's heart started to beat fast. He hated it when Martin bullied people. Li looked around him. He wished that someone would come by. He wished that someone would stop Martin. Most of all, Li wished that he was already home, eating his tea.

Everyone watched as Martin grabbed the boy's jacket.

"I want your money, kid!" shouted Martin.

"I've spent it," said the boy. His lip was wobbling. He was trying not to cry.

Li was getting worried. He looked at the others. They were all waiting to see what would happen.

Then Martin punched the boy hard in the chest.

**How is Li feeling**

**What would you do if you were Li**

Suddenly a car pulled up. The brakes screeched as it stopped. And out got Li's mum. She looked very red and very cross.

"Stop it, all of you!" said Li's mum loudly.

Everyone ran, Li's mum turned to the new boy, but he was already running through the park.

"Has this happened before?" Li's mum asked Li. He nodded.

"Get in!" snapped his mum. "Quickly!"

Li got into the car and clicked on his seat belt. His mum drove off. She sat up very straight and held the wheel tightly. Li didn't like the look on his mum's face. He didn't say a word.

Soon they were home. Li headed for his room.

"Stay here, Li!" said his mum, throwing down her bag. "I want to talk to you."

Li sat down quickly.

"I didn't know you were a bully!" said Li's mum. "I'm ashamed of you, Li."

**What do you think Li will say**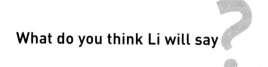

Li looked up at his mum. She was very upset.

"It wasn't my fault!" said Li. "Martin was the bully. I didn't do anything!"

"Exactly!" said Li's mum. "You didn't do anything to stop the bullying. That makes you a bully, too."

Is Li's mum right?

27

Li's mum sat down next to Li.

"When I was young, I was bullied," she told him.

"What happened?" asked Li.

"Two girls called me names and kicked me," said his mum. "A crowd of other girls stood watching. I kept hoping they would stop the bullies – but they didn't."

"I expect they were scared," said Li quietly.

"It is scary to stand up to bullies," agreed Li's mum. "But remember, most of the other boys feel just like you. They want the bullying to stop, too."

Li's mum smiled. "Who else looked unhappy about the bullying today?" she asked.

"Billy and John didn't like it," answered Li.

"Let's invite them both to tea," said Li's mum. "Let's all plan what to do next time Martin bullies."

Li nodded. "I could stand up to Martin if I wasn't on my own," he said.

"Great!" said Li's mum.

**What could Li and the others do to stop the bullying?**

## Feeling like Li

Li didn't like what Martin was doing. But he didn't try to stop him. Just watching didn't help. It made Li part of the bullying. And it probably made Martin feel more powerful.

## A bully in the group

Is there a bully in your group? Standing up to bullies isn't easy. You're afraid they'll start to pick on you. And, outside school, there are no teachers to tell. But don't let the bully keep the power. If there's a bully in your group, talk about it with your friends. Together, tell the bully to stop. If that doesn't work, ask a parent or a neighbour for help.

## Don't help bullies

Don't give bullies what they want. Don't give them sweets or money. And don't help them by keeping them secret. If you are being bullied – or know someone who is – tell an adult. Get the bullying stopped – today.

## Think about it

Michael, Sharon and Li were all bullies. And they each learnt something about bullying. Think about the stories in this book. What have you learnt about bullies – and about being bullied?

If you are feeling frightened or unhappy, don't keep it to yourself. Talk to an adult you can trust, like a parent or a teacher. If you feel really alone, you could telephone or write to one of these offices. Remember, there is always someone who can help.

**ABC Anti-Bullying Campaign**

Telephone 020 7378 1446

Address: 10 Borough High Street, London SE1 9QQ

(please send a stamped addressed envelope)

www.childline.org.uk

**Childline**

Freephone 0800 1111

Address: Freepost 1111, London N1 0BR

Childline for children in care

Freephone 0800 884444 (6 - 10pm).

**KIDSCAPE**

For advice on staying safe

152 Buckingham Palace Road, London SW1W 9TR

08451 205204. www.kidscape.org.uk

**NSPCC Child Protection Line**

Freephone 0808 8005000. www.nspcc.org.uk

**The Samaritans**

08457 909090. www.samaritans.org.uk